THE
AZTECS
Rise and Fall of a Great Empire

By Roger Smalley

Reading Consultant:
Timothy Rasinski, Ph.D.
Professor of Reading Education
Kent State University

Content Consultant:
Kimberly Gauderman
Assistant Professor of
Colonial Latin America
University of New Mexico

Red Brick™ Learning

Published by Red Brick™ Learning
7825 Telegraph Road, Bloomington, Minnesota 55438
http://www.redbricklearning.com

Library of Congress Cataloging-in-Publication Data
Smalley, Roger, 1947–
    The Aztecs : rise and fall of a great empire / by Roger Smalley.
    p. cm.
    Summary: Examines the birth, rise, and fall of the Aztec empire; its
cultural practices and religious beliefs, including human sacrifice; and
the Spaniards' eventual overthrow of the Aztecs.
Includes bibliographical references and index.
    ISBN 0-7368-2785-4 (hardcover)—ISBN 0-7368-2828-1 (pbk.)
    1. Aztecs—Juvenile literature. [1. Aztecs. 2. Indians of Mexico.]
    I. Title.
F1219.73.S57 2003
972'.018—dc21

                           2003005550

Created by Kent Publishing Services, Inc.
Designed by Signature Design Group, Inc.
This publisher has made every effort to trace ownership of all copyrighted
material and to secure necessary permissions. In the event of any questions
arising as to the use of any material, the publisher, while expressing regret for
any inadvertent error, will be happy to make necessary corrections.

Photo Credits:
Cover, page 15, Charles & Josette Lenars/Corbis; pages 4, 38, Archivo
Iconografico, S.A./Corbis; pages 6, 11, 12, 17, 35, Gianni Dagli Orti/Corbis;
page 18 (top) Burstein Collection, (bottom) Jeremy Horner/Corbis; page 25,
Werner Forman/Corbis; pages 27, 28, 31, 33, 39, 41, 43, Bettmann/Corbis; page
34, Hulton Archive/Getty Images; page 36, Danny Lehman/Corbis

Printed in the United States of America.

1 2 3 4 5 6 08 07 06 05 04 03

Table of Contents

An Aztec warrior in an Aztec village

— CHAPTER **1** —

Search for a New Home

A desert group looks for a new home. These people have put their trust in many gods. They believe these gods give them what they need to live. If they please their gods, they receive what they need. Now they need a new home. Surely, one of their gods will show them the way. They wait for a sign.

The Aztecs in the Desert

The story of the Aztecs (AZ-teks) begins in the 1200s. This desert people lived in what is now northern Mexico. Life was hard for the Aztecs. There was little food. They ate what they could find. They lived on rabbits, birds, lizards, snakes, and even **grubs**. The Aztecs knew which plants to eat as well.

---

grub: the larva of an insect; a short, fat worm

Aztec Gods

In the desert, water is **scarce**. The Aztecs prayed to their rain god, Tlaloc (TLAL-ok), to give them rain.

The Aztecs had other gods, too. They believed that gods made everything happen. The Aztecs thought the gods would help them if they gave them gifts of food, animals, cloth, and blood.

Some gods were more important to the Aztecs than others. One was the god of the wind. His name was Quetzalcoatl (ket-sal-ko-AHT-el). This god was also in charge of learning. He was shown as a snake with wings and feathers. Some said he had a white face with a beard.

A statue of the Aztec god Quetzalcoatl

---

scarce: hard to find

The War God

Huitzilopochtli (WIT-tzil-o-POCH-tlee), or "Hummingbird god," was the Aztec war god. The war god promised the Aztecs they would build a great **empire**. He promised he would show them where to build a new city. The Aztecs gave the war god many gifts. They thought he liked blood best. At first, they gave him animal blood. Then the Aztecs began to give him human blood and human hearts.

The Aztec god Huitzilopochtli

---

empire: a large area of land and people controlled by one government or ruler

Quetzalcoatl Is Angry

The Aztecs decided they should choose one god as most important. They chose the war god. They thought this made the wind god angry, so he left them and went east. Before he left, though, they believed Quetzalcoatl made a promise. He said that one day he would come back.

The Aztecs Find a New Land

The Aztecs looked for a place to build their city. They came to a valley between two mountains. The valley was filled with many lakes. Other people lived on the shores of the lakes.

One group gave the Aztecs land on the side of a volcano. For many years, the Aztecs grew stronger. Then they made a mistake. They killed a daughter of the king whose people gave them the land. They gave her blood and heart to their war god. When the king found out, he sent his army to destroy the Aztecs.

United States

Mexico

Mexico City
(Tenochtitlán)

GULF OF
MEXICO

• Tuxpan

Tenochtitlán ⬦

Aztec Empire

Coatzacoalcos •

Huaxyacac •
Tehuantepec •

PACIFIC
OCEAN

SCALE

100 ▮ km
▯ mi

Aztec Empire

The Aztecs Escape

The Aztecs ran to the shore of the biggest lake. Using wooden spears and shields, they made rafts. They floated out onto the lake and hid in some tall water plants. The Aztecs escaped the angry king's army. But now they had no home.

A War God's Promise

The Aztecs prayed to their war god. They asked the god to show them where to build a new city.

Suddenly, a huge eagle flew down from a nearby mountain. It flew over the Aztecs' heads and dove toward the ground. It then rose quickly with a snake in its claws. The eagle took the snake to the top of a **cactus** in the center of an island in the lake. The eagle then ate the snake.

---

cactus: a plant with scales or spines instead of leaves that grows in hot, dry places

The Aztecs were **amazed**! This was what they thought their war god had promised them. He had said that a snake with feathers and a cactus would show them where to build their new city. The island in the lake would be their new home!

The Aztecs could now stop searching. Their war god had shown them their new home. This island would be the start of a great city.

---

amaze: to surprise greatly

In this drawing, early Aztec leaders sit around the eagle and the cactus.

Aztecs build a block of land on the lake.

A Great City Rises

The Aztecs began to build a great city—right in the middle of a lake! How could they do this? What might this city look like? How would you plan such a city?

Building Up the Land

The island in the lake was too small to hold the Aztec city. So families began to **fence off** small areas in the lake. They filled in these areas to live on.

They did this by first pounding wood posts into the lake bottom. Using these posts, they built fences. Then they scooped grass, leaves, and mud into baskets and dumped this over the fences. In time, this built up to a small piece of land on which to live.

---

fence off: to enclose with a fence

A Large City

Soon there were thousands of these new blocks of land. The Aztecs called them *chinampas* (chi-NAHM-pas). The city of chinampas grew until it covered nearly 7 acres (2.8 hectares) of land.

The Aztecs left spaces between the chinampas. This made **canals**. Canals let people move around the city in canoes. The Aztecs could move heavy loads of food, stone, and wood by water.

Making Roads

The Aztecs built long roads that went from the center of the city across the lake to the shore. The roads also linked smaller islands.

To build the roads, the Aztecs piled rocks and dirt on the lake bottom. They covered the tops of these piles with flat stones to make roads. The lake waters came up to the roads on both sides. **Historians** now call these roads *causeways*.

---

canal: a strip of water boats use to cross stretches of land
historian: a person who is an expert in history

The painting, The Great Tenochtitlan, *by Diego Rivera, shows how the city was a group of islands joined by long roads.*

A Safe City

There were only a few causeways into the city. Aztecs would guard the causeways so other groups could not sneak across these roads and attack them.

The Aztecs also built bridges to connect the roads. Canoes could float under these bridges. The bridges could be cut down or burned if an enemy attacked. This made it very hard for an enemy to attack the city.

The Heart of the City

The Aztecs called their new city *Tenochtitlan* (tay-noch-TEET-lahn). In the center of the city was a great square. They built high walls around the square. The most important buildings stood inside these walls.

The largest buildings were stone **pyramids**. The tallest pyramid was more than 200 feet (61 meters) high. The Aztecs also built other, smaller pyramids with flat tops.

---

pyramid: a building with a square base and sloping sides

The great square also held the palaces of the king and his family, homes for the high priests, a ball court, and **warehouses** to store food, weapons, and treasures. Most of the buildings were white. But the temples were painted in beautiful colors of red, blue, yellow, and green.

From a small, swampy island, the Aztecs had built an amazing city. It had taken 200 years. But now they could enjoy life in their new home.

warehouse: a place where goods are stored

Model of the great square of the Aztec city, Tenochtitlan

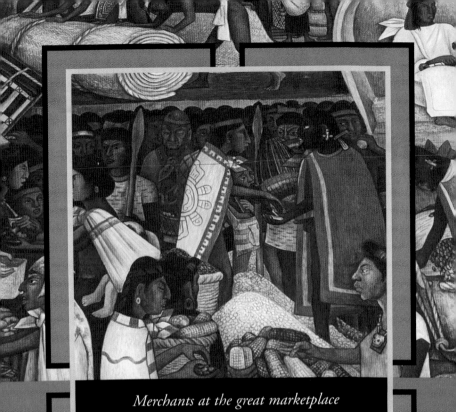

Merchants at the great marketplace

Basket of cacao pods

— CHAPTER **3** —

Aztec Life in Tenochtitlan

The Aztecs became a powerful group. Imagine life in their great island city. What do you think it was like? What problems do you think the Aztecs faced? How do you think they solved them?

The Lives of the People

Every day, the Aztec people came to the great **marketplace** near the city center. There they could buy or trade for things they needed. Instead of coins, the Aztecs used cacao (ca-CAY-oh) beans. Today, we use cacao beans to make chocolate.

> The Aztecs also used cacao beans to make a flavored drink. This very bitter drink was their favorite.

---

marketplace: an area where goods are sold

Daily Work

The people of the city did many kinds of work. Some made cloth, pottery, jewelry, or things of wood to sell at the market. Others worked at building homes, roads, and temples.

Aztec pottery

Family Life

After shopping for food and household items, such as pottery and cloth, the Aztecs would paddle their canoes home. Most houses were made of sun-dried bricks called *adobe* (uh-DOH-bee). Many had only one room. The family would cook, eat, and sleep together in this room.

Aztec women cared for their children and cooked. The women taught their daughters how to run a house. They taught them to grind corn into flour to make **tortillas** (tor-TEE-uhs). The women also gathered wild fruits and vegetables.

tortilla: a thin, baked pancake made from cornmeal

Most Aztec boys went to school. There they learned farming, fighting, and a **trade**. Boys from important families could become priests, judges, or leaders. Some girls were also highly trained and played important roles in **medicine**, farming, and trade.

A Water Problem

Like all great cities, Tenochtitlan had problems the Aztecs needed to solve. The water around the islands was not good to drink. As the city grew larger, the people needed more and more fresh water.

The Aztecs soon solved their water problem. They built a long road from the city to the lake shore and then up the side of a hill. They ended the road at a place where fresh springwater flowed out of the ground.

---

trade: a type of skilled job
medicine: the science of treating and preventing disease

Clean Water

To get the clean water to the city, the people built a square pipe. The pipe went from the spring into the city. This pipe was called an *aqueduct* (AH-kwuh-duhkt). The people brought jars to the end of the pipe. They filled them with fresh water. Then they took the water to their homes to use for drinking and cooking.

Aztec Fun

The Aztecs also took time out from work to have fun. Aztec children played with toys and dolls. They also played games and ran races. Adults had contests such as canoe races. Many men and boys went hunting. Some Aztecs played music, usually pipes and drums. Many special events included dancing.

Sports

Sometimes, the Aztecs watched teams play the game of *tlachtli* (TLACH-tlee). This game was played on a ball court made of stone. The center of the court was flat. The court had sloping walls around it, like a skateboard park. At the top of one wall, there was a stone hoop with a hole in the middle. The hoop was small and turned sideways. Players had to make a ball go through this hoop.

A tlachtli game

A Tough Game

The tlachtli ball was very hard. Players could not use their hands. They had to kick or hit the ball using their hips. Heavy pads on the hips, arms, and feet kept the players from being hurt. They also wore hard hats of leather and wood. Teams played until one side hit the ball through the hoop.

Sometimes, only two **warriors** played. This was a special game to **honor** the gods. The loser was put to death. The Aztecs thought a loser had **dishonored** the god he played for.

The Aztec Calendar

The Aztecs used a calendar based on the sun, moon, and stars. To keep track of time, they carved and painted a large, flat, round stone. The pictures on the stone stood for special days, years, and gods. The priests used the calendar to keep track of times when they needed to give gifts to the gods.

---

warrior: a person who fights in a war
honor: to show respect for
dishonor: to bring shame or disgrace on yourself or others

An Aztec calendar

Pleasing the Gods

The Aztecs had other special events to please the gods. In one, all lights and fires in the great city were put out. The priests led the people across the main causeway. Each person had a torch, but it was not lit. They made a long line from the center of the city, across the lake, and up the side of a mountain.

A Painful Fire

At a special place on the mountain, the priests put a man on his back on a large, flat stone. As the **star cluster** Pleiades (PLEE-uh-deez) moved above them, one priest came forward. He started a fire on the man's chest. Other priests held the man so he could not move.

One torch was lit from the fire on the man's chest. The fire was then passed from person to person. Soon a line of burning torches lit the road all the way to the city's center.

Lighting the Sun

The priests then cut open the man's chest. They used his blood to put out the fire. His heart was taken out. It was burned as a gift to the gods. The Aztecs thought this fire would keep the light of the sun burning. Then the world would not end.

---

star cluster: a group of stars

Strangers Approach

The Aztec people had settled into their new city. They worked and played. They raised their families and honored their gods. But soon, strangers would come to their city. What might they think of the Aztec way of life?

The Aztecs made human sacrifices to the sun.

Moctezuma II was the most famous Aztec king.

CHAPTER 4

Strangers Arrive

*The Aztecs had built a **thriving** city. But now strangers arrived in Tenochtitlan. Who were they? Were they friends or enemies? Were they gods? Why had they come?*

A Great King

There were 10 Aztec kings between 1325 and 1520. But the most well-known and respected was Moctezuma II (mok-te-ZU-mah).

Moctezuma II was a great warrior. He also knew the history of his people. He knew the stories of the **jealous** god Quetzalcoatl. He thought Quetzalcoatl might one day return to destroy the Aztecs. Moctezuma II lived with great doubts and fears.

---

thriving: successful
jealous: wanting what someone else has

A Sign in the Sky

Moctezuma asked his people to tell him if they saw anything strange. For 10 years, the people watched. Volcanoes erupted. There were great storms and floods. Once, an earthquake shook the city.

One night, a ball of fire appeared in the sky. It came out of the east and got bigger every night. The flames of the fireball looked like feathers. It had a long tail behind it like a snake. The Aztecs did not know this was a **comet**. They thought it was a sign of bad things to come.

More News!

Then, one day in 1519, a man ran into Moctezuma's throne room. He told the king a wild story. He had seen strange men coming from the east. They came in great boats that moved without paddles. Big pieces of cloth hung above each boat.

---

comet: a frozen mass of dust and gas that moves through space

The strangers had strong weapons that could kill with a loud noise. Some strangers rode on giant, four-legged beasts that could run very fast. Their leader looked like Quetzalcoatl. He had white skin and a beard. He was leading his men to Tenochtitlan.

The king believed this leader might be the god Quetzalcoatl. He sent men with gold to meet him. The gold had been Quetzalcoatl's at the time the god left in anger.

The Aztecs asked the strangers to take the gold and go away. But seeing the gold, the strangers wanted even more to come to the city. Moctezuma was worried. Was the wind god coming back from the east to destroy the Aztecs?

Quetzalcoatl

The Strangers

The man Moctezuma thought might be a god was a Spanish soldier named Hernan Cortes (er-NAN kor-TEHZ). The Spanish governor of Cuba had sent Cortes to explore the coast of what is now Mexico. Cortes had heard about the Aztec city and the gold. He and his men wanted that gold.

An Army Arrives

Cortes had a small army. They were soon joined by thousands of other **native** peoples who disliked the Aztecs. The Spanish soldiers wore **armor** and carried guns and swords. They also had cannons and horses. The Aztecs had never seen these things before.

The Aztecs had one more reason to fear Cortes. He arrived the year their king thought the wind god might return.

---

native: belonging to a certain place
armor: a covering worn to protect the body in battle

Moctezuma Welcomes Cortes

The Spanish soldiers and the native peoples with them crossed the mountains and came to the lake edge. They saw the huge Aztec city with its canals, causeways, and pyramids.

Moctezuma came to meet Cortes. He was carried in a special chair. No one was allowed to touch the king. The Aztecs believed anyone who touched Moctezuma would die.

Cortes and Moctezuma talked. Then, Cortes hugged Moctezuma. The Aztecs were amazed Cortes did not die! The king also thought only a god could touch him. Was Cortes a god? Was he Quetzalcoatl? The king welcomed Cortes and his men into the city.

Cortes meets Moctezuma.

Cortes Becomes Angry

Moctezuma and Cortes talked for many months. One day, Cortes went into the temple of the war god. There he saw the blood and human hearts from **sacrifices**. He became angry at the Aztecs for these killings.

An Aztec sacrifice

sacrifice: something given to the gods

The Fighting Begins

Cortes took the king **prisoner**. The Aztecs then circled the palace and would not let the Spanish leave. Moctezuma asked the Aztecs to let Cortes go. But the warriors were angry with their king because he had welcomed the strangers. They threw stones. One hit Moctezuma in the head.

Later, the Aztec king died. It is not clear how he died. While the Aztecs buried their king, the Spanish tried to steal the Aztec gold and leave the city.

The Aztecs now knew the Spanish were not gods. They were men who wanted to steal their gold! The Aztecs wanted to kill the strangers who had tricked them.

---

prisoner: a person who is held against his or her will

Eagle-shaped container used for sacrificed hearts

A statue of an Aztec eagle warrior

Chapter 5

The Aztec Empire Ends

Imagine you are a young Aztec warrior. Strangers have come into your city and are robbing your people. The strangers are strong, but you are brave. Your name is Cazcatli (kahz-CAHT-lee). This is your story.

An Aztec Warrior's Story

The strangers who came to your city many months ago seemed friendly at first. But now, they have taken your king prisoner. They are trying to flee the city with their pockets stuffed with gold. A battle is going on.

You paddle toward the battle in a canoe. The rain and darkness make it hard to see clearly. You hear the screams of men fighting and dying.

The Battle Is Won?

Your canoe reaches the causeway. You grab your war club and sharp stone knife. You jump from the boat and join the fighting.

The strangers are good fighters. One of them swings his sword at your head. You duck just in time. You hit your club into the stranger's knee. He screams and falls down. Your knife moves fast, and the stranger is dead. Your fellow warriors come at the enemy from all sides. There are too many of you. The strangers try to run away.

An Aztec warrior

Some of the strangers have filled their pockets with gold. Gold is very heavy. It slows them down. They fall off the causeway and into the lake. The heavy gold drags them to the bottom. They cannot swim back up.

You see that you are winning, and you fight harder. A small group of the enemy escapes down the road. Others are quickly killed or captured. You have won the battle!

The Aztecs fight the Spanish.

The Great City Is Destroyed

This warrior's story does not end with Aztec victory, however. Cortes got away and returned to his ships. There he found more Spanish explorers and soldiers. He showed them the Aztec gold. They joined Cortes and he led them back to the city.

While Cortes was gone, many Aztecs became sick from **smallpox**. The Spanish had brought this **disease** with them. It had never appeared among the Aztecs before. Many Aztecs died of smallpox.

Too Much Firepower

Warriors of other peoples joined Cortes and his new army. The Aztecs had built their empire by fighting their neighbors. Sometimes, they had used them as human sacrifices. Many of these neighbors wanted to see the Aztecs destroyed. They were happy to join the Spanish against the Aztecs.

---

smallpox: a disease that causes blisters on the skin and often leads to death
disease: a sickness or illness

Cortes returned and attacked Tenochtitlan in 1521. His men had built boats with flat bottoms and put cannons on them. Day after day, the cannons blew apart the buildings in the great city.

At last, the Spanish captured Cuauhtemoc (kwa-oow-TAY-mock), the new Aztec king. The fighting stopped. The Aztecs' great city and their empire were gone forever.

Cortes' men destroy the city.

41

Epilogue

How We Know

How do we know about the Aztecs? They wrote using pictures in books called *codices* (KOH-deh-seez). Although most codices are gone, a few remain. Also, we can look at the carvings the Aztecs made on their buildings. Many of these carvings tell us stories about Aztec life.

The Spanish also wrote about the Aztecs. So did other native groups who knew them. But we can't always trust these sources. Remember, the Aztecs had many enemies.

There are still Aztecs living in Mexico today. They are proud of the part they played in Mexico's history. In fact, the name *Mexico* comes from the Spanish name for the Aztecs, *Mexica* (may-SHEE-kah). Today, every time we say "Mexico," we are really saying, "The Land of the Aztecs."

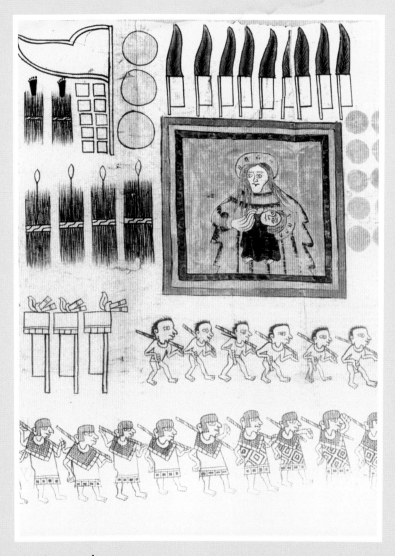

An Aztec codex

Glossary

amaze: to surprise greatly

armor: a covering worn to protect the body in battle

cactus: a plant with scales or spines instead of leaves that grows in hot, dry places

canal: a strip of water boats use to cross stretches of land

comet: a frozen mass of dust and gas that moves through space

disease: a sickness or illness

dishonor: to bring shame or disgrace on yourself or others

empire: a large area of land and people controlled by one government or ruler

fence off: to enclose with a fence

grub: the larva of an insect; a short, fat worm

historian: a person who is an expert in history

honor: to show respect for

jealous: wanting what someone else has

marketplace: an area where goods are sold

medicine: the science of treating and preventing disease

native: belonging to a certain place

prisoner: a person who is held against his or her will

pyramid: a building with a square base and sloping sides

sacrifice: something given to the gods

scarce: hard to find

smallpox: a disease that causes blisters on the skin and often leads to death

star cluster: a group of stars

thriving: successful

tortilla: a thin, baked pancake made from cornmeal

trade: a type of skilled job

warehouse: a place where goods are stored

warrior: a person who fights in a war

Bibliography

Gonzalbo, Pablo Escalante. *A Day with an Aztec.* Minneapolis: Runestone Press, a division of Lerner Publishing Group, 2000.

Hull, Robert. *The Aztecs.* The Ancient World. Austin, Texas: Raintree/Steck-Vaughn, 1998.

Kimmel, Eric A. *Montezuma and the Fall of the Aztecs.* New York: Holiday House, 2000.

Macdonald, Fiona. *You Wouldn't Want to Be an Aztec Sacrifice!* New York: Franklin Watts, 2001.

Rees, Rosemary. *The Aztecs.* Understanding People in the Past. Chicago: Heinemann Library, 1999.

Tanaka, Shelley. *Lost Temple of the Aztecs: What It Was Like When the Spaniards Invaded Mexico.* New York: Hyperion Press, 2000.

Useful Addresses

The Great Temple Museum
No. 8 Seminario Street
The Zocalo
Mexico City, Mexico

National Museum of Anthropology
Paseo de la Reforma Ave. & Gandhi St.
Chapultepec Forest
Mexico City, Mexico

Internet Sites

Ancientmexico.com
http://www.ancientmexico.com

Aztecs
http://www.42explore.com/aztec.htm

The Aztecs/Mexicas
http://www.indians.org/welker/aztec.htm

Index